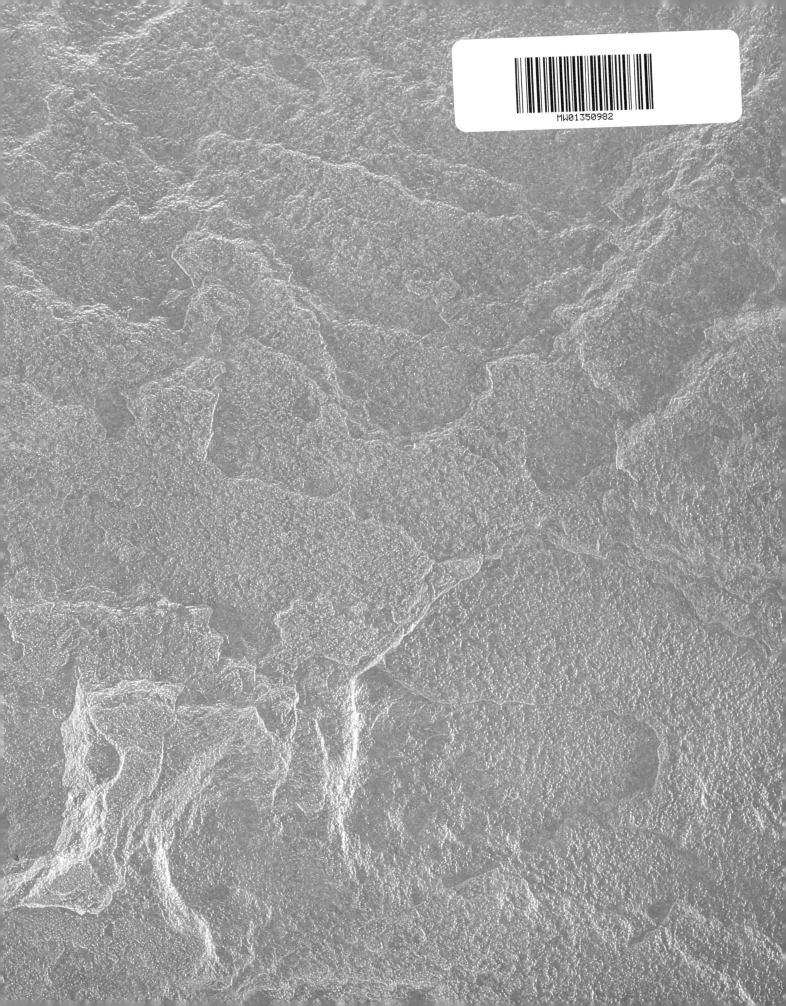

LAKSHMI LAL

INDIA BOOK HOUSE PVT LTD

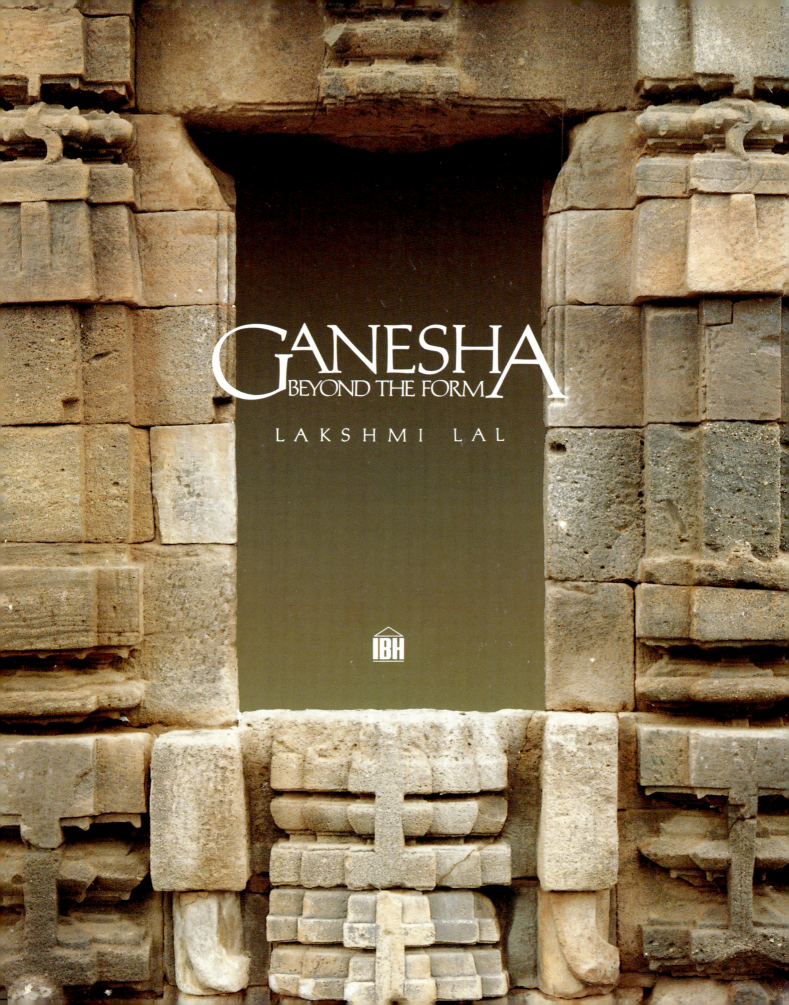

Free renderings of Vedic verses by Lakshmi Lal

The author gratefully acknowledges the guidance of Dr. G. H. Godbole through the mazes of Ganesha worship.

## PHOTO CREDITS

**Satish Parab**
*8, 14, 24, 29, 35, 38, 48, 62, 70, 86, 90, 102, 104*

**Jagdish Agarwal / Dpa**
*10*

**D Banerjee / Dpa**
*27*

**Dayaram A Chavda / Dpa**
*34, 42, 45(left), 47, 52, 57, 66, 67(right), 98*
From the Swali Family Collection

**Anil A Dave / Dpa**
*2, 21, 43*

**J A Hedao / Dpa**
*46*

**B P Maiti / Dpa**
*20*

**S Mehta / Dpa**
*68*

**Satish T Parashar / Dpa**
*33, 73 (right)*

**G C Patel / Dpa**
*40*

**Suraj N Sharma / Dpa**
*51(left), 73(left), 75, 81*

**Aman Nath & Francis Wacziarg**
*4, 51(left), 83*

**Samar S Jodha**
*16, 26, 28, 30*
From the Aman Nath Collection

**Photostock**
*59, 64*

**Gopi Kukde**
*6, 18*

**Jagdish Haralankar**
*67(left), 96, 100*

**K B Jothady**
*74*

**Courtesy: Harsh Neotia (Conclave Art Collection)**
*41, 45(right), 54, 65*

ISBN 81-85028-05-2

© INDIA BOOK HOUSE PVT LTD
*First printed 1991*
*Reprinted 1995*

*Illustration and Design*
Gopi Kukde

*Processing*
Unique Photo Offset Services
Bombay

*Printing*
Krishna Art Printery
Bombay

*Published by*
INDIA BOOK HOUSE PVT LTD
Mahalaxmi Chambers, 5th Floor,
22, Bhulabhai Desai Road
Bombay 400 026

*All rights reserved*

written for
kaverimutta, kamu
and
gajendra

# CONTENTS

**10** Introduction

**12** The Beginning

**22** Born Again and Again

**36** Beyond the Symbol

**60** Om Ganeshaya Namah

**84** A Travel Story

गणानां त्वा गणपतिं हवामहे ।
कविं कवीनामुपमश्रवस्तमम् ॥
ज्येष्ठराजं ब्रह्मणां ब्रह्मणस्पत ।
आ नः शृण्वन्नूतिभिः सीद सादनम् ॥

Chief amongst all groups, lord of them all
Of all wise ones, the wisest yet
In name and fame, beyond compare
Prime cause supreme of all our prayers
We invoke you, favour us.
Pray be seated, hear us, Lord.

— Rig Veda

*INTRODUCTION*

A god is man's idea of an answer to all problems. Since, moreover, problems never come singly, a ranging pantheon is a sensible approach to life. Ganesha sits snugly ensconced in a pantheon that is designed for the business of living – and praying. Life calls for resilience and the Indian subcontinental consciousness has seen to it that neither Ganesha nor the pantheon remained fixed and immovable.

A good idea grows. From a simple primitive spirit and godling who began life probably as the animal totem of a Dravidian tribe, he changed form and substance to reach the very inner circle of the major Indian gods; for no undertaking, no worship, no rites save the funeral, start without homage to him, remover of all obstacles from the path to success.

Good ideas also travel. Ganesha has travelled far and wide – to Nepal, Tibet, Burma, Indo-China, Thailand, Borneo, Java, Bali and as far east as China and Japan, on the backs of both Hinduism and Buddhism. Like any good idea, he has taken kindly to change, allowing each country to do with him as it will. He is a transnational, transcultural, pan-religious divinity.

And, of course, like the best ideas, he makes a good story, a tale told by India, "the story-teller of the world". Old in the ways of wisdom, India has always known that few things teach like a story.

Ganesha is everywhere — in temples, in wayside shrines, in homes; but nearest and dearest of all, in the warmth and closeness of your heart, in the truth of your own consciousness, your Self. He is the *antaryami*, part and parcel of your innermost being.

The Indian spiritual journey is inward and Self-centred. Ganesha, like the good god that he is, takes you by the hand and leads you right into the vast expanse of the little space within each human heart, the *hridayi akasha* of Indian religious philosophy. Within that enclosure of the spirit, individual and cosmic at the same time, even as the devotee witnesses the miracle, he will vanish, leaving only the experience, the *anubhava* of *moksha* or release. Until then, which is usually a long and difficult way off, the form, the God, is all.

Glory be to Ganesha — quaint, grotesque, awesome and utterly lovable — sitting, standing or dancing as he centres the gravity of his burdensome belly, with the swaying grace of the elephant.

# THE BEGINNING

त्वं आनन्दमयस्त्वम् ब्रह्ममयः।
त्वं चलासि वाक्पदानि॥

*Speech in all its ways you are*
*The sound, the silence of the word*
*The echo deep within that leads*
*To bliss of Brahman Absolute.*

— Atharva Veda

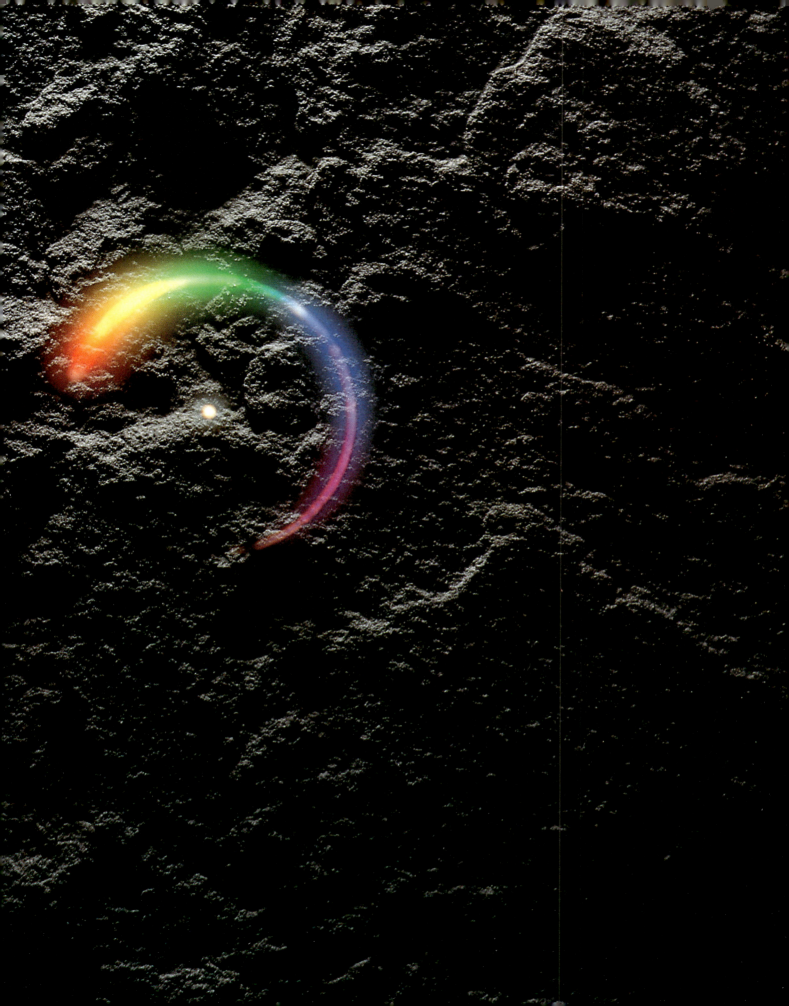

he wheel of Time had gathered speed and settled into the steady hum of the Dravidian era. Here, somewhere between fact and vision, legend and myth, in the hidden interstices of historicity, scholarly speculation sights the first clues to Ganesha. We have the elephant totem of a Dravidian tribe, and a Dravidian solar deity imaged as the elephant-power of daylight, overpowering and mounting the cornered rat of darkness. Ganesha is even now shown with the sun-god Surya, and in Nepal he is born, not of Shiva and Parvati, but of a ray of sunshine, as Surya-Ganapati.

Moving forward into Vedic times, we come across a hymn to Dantin (the 'tusked' or 'toothed' one). Here again one turns to scholarly guesswork. The commentator Sayana provides an elephant face for Dantin when he mentions a *tunda* (nose, proboscis, trunk) – one of Ganesha's names is Vakratunda (he of the curved trunk). The Rig Veda mentions a Ganapati who was Shiva himself or, according to one opinion, an aspect of Shiva; and aspects, as we know, have a way of detaching themselves and growing into related but independent divinities.

A definite trail has now been laid from totem or deity to an animistic cult. The god now begins, literally, to take on form

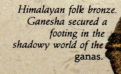

*Himalayan folk bronze. Ganesha secured a footing in the shadowy world of the ganas.*

and assume a name – in other words, to manifest himself. Legends, mainly Puranic, begin to gather round him, conferring both status and identity. Ganesha, emerging from a primal background, was looking for a step up the divine evolutionary ladder. He gets a footing – in the shadowy world of the *ganas*. They were Shiva's motley crew of attendants, grotesque, misshapen, near-human beings. Given his size, shape and cast of countenance – some *ganas* had animal heads – Ganesha slipped neatly into this category.

The *ganas* were not as lowly as they seemed at first glance. They were Shiva's favoured retinue, roaming the Himalayan slopes with few to challenge either them or their master's might. They were warriors, musicians, dancers; and rubbed shoulders with the *yakshas*, a rotund lot of sylvan spirits, wealthy neighbours, who were the attendants of Kubera, god of wealth and inseparable companion of Shiva. Though there is no actual link with the *yakshas*, there is a touch of the jungle spirit in Ganesha's get-up and a distinct physical correspondence – the squat rotundity. From animal to forest-and-mountain creature to the inner conclave of Shiva's mountain complex, and finally into the bosom of the holy family itself. It was a triumphal progression.

There is one more ancestral strain in Ganesha's genes, one which was to surface as an important aspect of his personality – the *vinayakas*. They were a malevolent group, hangers-on of Shiva, a tribe of malignant spirits conducive to appeasement, controlling common dangers and ailments and threats – 280 of them, shortlisted to eight, then four, and finally reduced by Shiva to one composite form – Vinayaka. We now have with us, clearly sketched, Ganapati-Vinayaka, the future lord of Shiva's *gana*-hordes and the lord of obstacles. These remained his two major functions or aspects.

There is an interesting variant interpretation of Ganapati. Ananda Coomaraswamy, eminent art-historian, takes the word 'gana' to represent lists of related works and classifications. The concept of numbers and groupings (*gana*) is the foundation of worldly existence. Hence Ganesha could well be 'lord of categories'. Categorising is an essential human function. It is what introduces order into chaos and makes the world a manageable place to live in.

Ekadanta (his earliest Sanskrit name), Ganapati, Vinayaka is now out in the open, on a heavenly platform. He only needs supportive legends for a full-fledged launch into the main pantheon – and that was a mere matter of time and a fertile religious imagination. We have the basic

plan: elephant-faced, single-tusked, *gana*-like and corpulent. Alfred Foucher describes this long wait and final entry in picturesque terms: '...by then (5th or 6th century A.D.) the elephant-god had already behind him century upon century, if not thousands of years, of silent waiting at the foot of the sacred tree of the pre-Aryan village, standing on the roughly built platform which he shared with the other rustic deities; with the snakes which were to give birth to many Naga-kings, with the monkey which was to become Hanuman, with the vulture which would later grow into Garuda ... For these ... were so deeply rooted in an unfathomable past that the aristocracy of the new gods, introduced by the immigrant Aryans, were compelled to adopt them in some form or other.'

Ganapati's career was a chequered but satisfactory one, a steady plod to success. Like the elephant who seems to swerve, but is only swaying in a straight line, he makes it to his goal with unhurried grace. He rose from the ranks to hold high office in the best possible manner, through repeated and popular demand, beginning with his mother. She struck a bargain with Shiva for his life as well as his post as chief of the *ganas*. The gods repeatedly clamoured for his creation, to remove obstacles from the path of the righteous and to place hindrances in the path of the unrighteous.

He filled a recurring need – the judicious control and manipulation of the stumbling block. It was a mundane and irksome job, beyond the pale of the major gods and the sages. The gods were occupied with grandiose schemes, and the sages were preoccupied with matters of enlightenment and salvation. Ganesha was an aspiring god who happened to be in the right place at the right time.

Why he was born dazzlingly beautiful only to be disfigured, in most cases by his own parents, is one of mythology's unsolved mysteries. It could be an atavistic clinging to animal worship; equally, a wholesome respect for and acceptance of the animal world and a desire to pay it the ultimate tribute of divinity. It might just possibly be an indulgence in the aesthetic of the absurd, a stroke of elephantine humour. We shall never know.

# BORN AGAIN AND AGAIN

त्वमेव प्रत्यक्षं तत्त्वमसि । त्वमेव केवलं कर्तासि ।
त्वमेव केवलं धर्तासि । अवतु त्वं माम् । त्वमेव केवलं हर्तासि ।
...त्वं साक्षादात्मासि नित्यम् ॥
ऋतं वच्मि । सत्यं वच्मि ॥

*You are Creator, you and you alone*
*You are Preserver, you and you alone*
*You are Destroyer, you and you alone*
*You are Self eternal, you and you alone*
*You are Truth perceived indeed, and manifest*
*These facts I state, this truth I speak*
*May you bless me and protect.*
  *— Atharva Veda*

**G**anesha was born many times – and many legends – over. Most gods come gift-wrapped in layers of myth; but Ganesha's cross-Puranic nativity stories speak of a strange and primal vision. The earth-dirt of his mother's body, the waters of his aunt Ganga, the fire and air of his father's mind and the ether of his cosmic consciousness. He has a truly elemental lineage.

As for parentage, he was born of each separately and of the two jointly; indirectly, Ganga, as the one who awakened him to life in one myth, could have laid claim to him, as also Malini, an elephant-headed demoness who wandered the banks of the Ganga.

He belonged to all of them, and to none of them. He was common, extraordinary property.

Most stories about Ganesha's birth are centred around situations in which the *devas* (gods), threatened with the growing power of the *asuras* (anti-gods), appeal to Shiva for the creation of a counterforce, a being who could obstruct and check them. It was usually a crisis calling for immediate action and, of course, an instantaneous birth. Disaster management, in short.

In our first story, we have the *asuras* in an uncharacteristic role. Encouraged by Shiva, they performed ceremonies and

Seated on a tiger skin, Shiva filters bhang. Kangra painting, 19th century.

rites that earned them, perforce, his goodwill and blessings. Armed with these powers they fought with the gods, disturbing the peace of the heavens and threatening their very existence. Indra, chief of the gods, appealed to Shiva who, since he could not retract boons already granted, had to create a being who could waylay and deflect the marauders. Marshalling his creative powers and helped by Parvati, he succeeded. Ganesha was born, a handsome young man and as Ganapati, leader of the *ganas*, he set to work at once. The *asuras* retreated, and the gods had the heavens to themselves once again.

One day, another story goes, the gods and the sages sat down to compare notes on their various activities, and to consult with one another on future courses of action. They soon realised that all was not justice and fairplay in the universe. Those doing good work had to face many problems and surmount unforeseen obstacles, while those who led wicked, heedless lives seemed to proceed, unhampered. This imbalance had to be corrected and the answer seemed to be the advent of a new god who would go about judiciously standing in the way of the unrighteous and equally conscientiously clearing the path for the righteous.

They went to their only refuge, Shiva. The lord sensed their problems even before they had voiced them. Glancing at Parvati, his face glowed with the thought of the birth-to-be, as it flashed through his cosmic mind. In that magic moment of mystery, a dazzling young man with the qualities of Shiva himself appeared. Seeing the unsettling effect that his beauty had on the heavenly damsels gathered there and even on herself, Parvati cried out: 'May you have an elephant's head and protruding belly!' Of course, the blessings followed, from both father and mother, pronouncing him lord and controller of all obstacles and the first of all deities to be worshipped in any ceremony.

It was Shiva again who was responsible for another situation, and another story, by blessing and granting boons to the unworthy. They were now crowding the heavens, offending the gods with their uncouth ways. Once more, the obvious solution presented itself. Ganesha had to be born to obstruct, hamper and generally regulate the flow of traffic to heaven, keeping undesirable elements out. This time, Shiva directed the gods to Parvati for he had run out of ideas. She gently rubbed her body, and like fire out of the sacrificial fuel-sticks when they are rubbed together,

there swayed into sight an elephant-headed, four-armed being. Parvati, addressing him as husband of Buddhi (wisdom) and Siddhi (success), explained to him the delicate nature of his mission.

Yet another legend is born, as Ganesha waits in the wings ready to appear. Shiva himself related it to his son Ganesha. He was conceived in as normal a manner as family traditions would permit. Shiva and Parvati, wandering the forests, at peace with each other and with the world in flower, watched two elephants make love. It was an impressive sight and they were struck with the grace and majesty of their spectacular mating games. They decided to turn into elephants and of that whimsical, sportive union was born their elephant-headed elder son.

In one manifestation he was Krishna himself. Parvati, childless, prayed to Shiva, pleading piteously. She worshipped him with fruits, flowers and fervent incantations. A whole year had passed in severe penance, with no results. Just when she had given up all hope, an aerial voice ordered her to retire to her bedchamber where she found a beautiful boy. To celebrate the event, she invited all the gods and planets to a feast. Among them was the malevolent planet Shani (Saturn), who however kept his eyes firmly lowered so as not to blight the newborn child. Parvati in the first flush of motherhood reproached him for not admiring her baby and Shani raised his eyes. The child's head fell off and there was consternation all round. Vishnu, mounting Garuda, flew to a far-off lake where he found Indra's elephant, Airavata and his son. Chopping one of their heads off (it is not clear whose), he rushed back and saved the situation. Followers of the Krishna-Ganapati cult worship images of the infant Ganesha crawling in the classic baby-Krishna style, holding a *modaka* in place of the customary ball of fresh butter. The sect even appropriated the Bhagavad Gita, substituting Ganesha's name for Krishna's.

From one strange birth to another. Parvati, while bathing, mixed oils, potions and the dirt scraped off her own body and offered it to an elephant-headed demoness, Malini who lived on the banks of the river Ganga. Swallowing the mixture, she gave birth to a male child with five elephant-heads. Shiva reduced the five heads to one and before disputes could arise regarding motherhood, arbitrarily declared the child to be Parvati's!

A variation of this legend also exists. Parvati fashioned an elephant-headed image out of bathing oils, ointment and the dirt of her body. Sprinkling it with water from the Ganga, she brought Ganesha to life.

Shiva's mind was a powerful instrument of creation – he was not just a phallic force. According to an ancient Tantric text he had six heads and six minds, thus expanding his mental faculties to gargantuan proportions. Four heads faced the four cardinal points, with the fifth placed above and the sixth below, hidden and unseen. From the head facing west, termed Kama (desire), emerged the gods Krishna, Ganesha, Yama, the sun, the moon and other planets.

As a single parent, Shiva compounds the Ganesha mystique, making of it an ideation, a metaphysic, an abstraction, as we shall see from the following story.

The gods were as usual in trouble, waiting to be rescued; and of course, only Shiva knew how. It struck him while looking at Uma that there was a niche available and waiting for the new god – all the elements held the impress of his form except one, the sky. It must have been an oversight, and the thought made him laugh out loud. Of that burst of echoing laughter, using Brahma's guidelines for creating a sentient being, and his own self-knowing powers, he produced Ganesha, a veritable Rudra, cast in his own image. The boy excited his jealousy, and like Parvati in another legend, he cursed him, giving him an elephant-head, a pot-belly and a crawling serpent for his sacred thread. It was quite an obstacle for Ganesha to overcome, this misshapen form wished upon him by his own parents.

The best known legend is also the most interesting. It shows the divine couple squabbling, Parvati standing up for her rights, protesting against repeated invasions of her privacy by a thoughtless husband; and Shiva, incensed and taken by surprise, fighting to win. The conflict hardens into a divine tussle of wills, taking on cosmic proportions as god after god gets drawn in, only to face defeat and humiliation. Even the Creator was not spared.

It all started with a relatively minor issue, as such things usually do. Parvati's companions advised her to acquire her own personal guard. Her husband Shiva had the habit of walking in without warning — very sensibly, they had separate living quarters. She had already been surprised once in her bath. After all, her friends said, his attendants, Nandi and the others, were bound to be slack where her needs and comforts were concerned.

It happened again. Shiva seemed to have no respect for her privacy. Scrubbing herself in her bath one day, she snapped out of a pleasant reverie, resolving to create her own son, there and then, and appoint him guardian of her suite of rooms. She did not have to go far for the stuff of life. From the dust and dirt that came off her body, she created a beautiful young man, Ganapati, blessed him and gave him the staff of authority.

The expected soon happened. Shiva, as was his habit, arrived unannounced when Parvati was in her bath, and the young man stopped him. Shiva tried to push past him but Ganesha barred the way. Shiva tried to reason, then argued and threatened and finally withdrew in a huff, putting his *ganas* on the job of humbling the upstart

Shiva and his family. Label printed by textile company, Manchester, which was pasted on bales of cloth exported to India during the 19th century.

guard. They came to blows and the matter grew out of all proportion.

The gods were beaten back as Ganesha taunted them. The great Brahma even had his beard and moustache tweaked! Vishnu had to withdraw twice – and all this while Narada, the trouble-shooting world-wandering, busybody of a sage went from one camp to the other, fanning tempers and whipping up the rising fury of the already furious combatants. Narada was in his element. Here was much mischief to be made! It was a heaven-sent opportunity. The heavenly hordes had gathered to watch. Sparks flew from the clash of egos larger than life, getting larger by the minute as attitudes hardened.

Parvati learning from Narada that her son was besieged, created two terrible *shaktis* – one came, open mouth dark with destruction and the other followed, mowing down bodies with death-dealing flashes of lightning. Just when all seemed lost, Narada suggested that Shiva kill Ganesha, which he finally did, with his trident. The error was compounded. Parvati was inconsolable and threatened to flood the world. Again, just in time, she was appeased by Narada and truce was declared. Shiva sent his *ganas* northwards to fetch the head of the first living creature sighted. An elephant's head was brought and joined to Ganesha's body and Shiva,

through Vedic chanting, infused him with his own life-giving energies. The youth stood up, accepting overlordship of the *ganas* from his father who also declared him Remover of Obstacles and the first to be worshipped in all ceremonies.

These were by no means all his births. He would appear periodically on earth, followed by local legend, whenever his presence was needed to rid the earth of demons and devils.

Ganesha is a unique God. Blessed with many births in the same lifetime, multi-sourced and multi-formed, he grew in status to overtake all the gods as prime mover. He gained total Vedic-Aryan respectability while proudly retaining his primal Dravidian lineage. He adapted, literally, without losing face.

# BEYOND THE SYMBOL

गणादिं पूर्वमुच्चार्य वर्णादिंतदनन्तरम् ।
अनुस्वारः परतरः अर्धेन्दुलसितम् ।
तारेण ऋद्धम् एतत्तव अनुस्वरूपम्...गँ...

Utter 'ga' the consonant
Of the alphabet the first
Follow next with vowel 'a'
And after that the nasal dot
Enhanced with curve of crescent moon:
This is you, your unique sound
Your mantra, 'gan'...

— Atharva Veda

Naming is a serious business in India, not merely an important rite of passage marked by a ceremony. It is intended to give you a distinct aura and stand guard over your behaviour, your demeanour, your bearing; it forms you. It might even motivate you. Your parents choose your name, and you live up to it.

A god has many names. Each name hints at his physical appearance, attributes, insignia, mount, banner or pennant, function, personality, temperament, life-history — in fact, his profile. The name, literally, leads you into the form that is the deity, his or her manifest being. After all, the whole universe and creation itself hinges on the pairing of name (*nama*) with form (*rupa*). The metaphysical concept of *nama-rupa* defines the manifest universe. When the unmanifest, the supreme Truth, manifests itself, as it does cyclically, it can only do so by bringing into play names and forms. And we must remember that the pantheon, though divine and immortal, is as much part of the manifest universe as we mortals are. With them too it is the name-form unit around which the ego, the I-ness, the very essence of individuation, deposits itself.

A string of Ganesha's names, and there are many such lists, stands for a particular concept, becomes a particular sketch. The following list is from a hymn that is only an enumeration of twelve of his names. When meditated upon, it conjures up a generally accepted and popular picture of Ganesha:

| | |
|---|---|
| Vakratunda | : with curved trunk |
| Ekadanta | : single-tusked |
| Krishnapingaksha | : with dark brown eyes |
| Gajavaktra | : elephant-mouthed |
| Lambodara | : pot-bellied |
| Vikata | : disfigured |
| Vighnaraja | : King of Obstacles |
| Dhumravarna | : smoke-coloured |
| Bhalachandra | : (wearing) the crescent moon |
| Vinayaka | : Lord of Obstacles |
| Ganapati | : Lord of Shiva's *ganas* |
| Gajanana | : elephant-faced |

*Painting by Ganesh Pyne. Contemporary.*

As we can see, the list is quite an adequate, even comprehensive projection, if the devotee fills in the gaps while meditating. It outlines a physical form as well as suggests or reminds one of the underlying symbolism. The curved trunk stands for the zig-zig path to wisdom. Depending on which way it turns, it represents the beaten (right and sanctified) and off-beat (left or Tantric) paths to salvation. The elephant-mouth and face hark back to his totem-pole, animist, jungle origins; the single tusk speaks of strength and power, or unity as opposed to duality; the pot-belly, as capacious as space itself, is full to bursting with wisdom (the *modakas*, or sweets, that he is constantly eating); or alternately, with the seeds of all life. Coloured smoke-grey for the Kaliyuga, his forehead is lit by the crescent moon, linking him both with his father, Shiva, and a legend. One dark night, Ganesha looked round for the moon and found him drained of all his lustre, weeping disconsolately – a sage's curse had reduced him to this plight, he said. Ganesha picked him up and placed him on his forehead, and he revived instantly, glowing once again with renewed light and life.

There are many different lists of Ganesha's names. Put together they would make a Ganesha tapestry, a multi-coloured prayer-mat worked with all the skeins of Ganesha worship.

*Mayureshwar.*
*Painting on glass,*
*Rajasthan,*
*19th century.*

## Form

A god takes form and shape in the collective unconscious of a group of people sharing a common culture. As stated before, name and form interact in a continuing process which gradually begins to stabilise. Image-making and iconography follow; rules and guidelines gradually crystallise through custom, tradition and sacred texts. The deity begins to get established.

Ganesha is a god, it is said, with the largest number of variant forms. A Puranic verse prepares us for this when it states that Ganapati's form changes according to the *yuga* or era in which he manifests – an instance of divine resilience, not to say commonsense! As Vinayaka in the first or *krita yuga*, he is ten-armed, lustrous and rides a lion. As Mayureshwara in the second or *treta yuga* he is six-armed, white and rides a peacock. As Gajanana in the third or *dvapara yuga*, he is four-armed, red and rides a rat. As Dhumraka in the last or *kali yuga*, he is two-armed and smoke-grey.

As early as the fifth or sixth century A.D. the iconographic form of Ganesha had got well set. The first definitive, sculptural images of Ganesha as a god also appear around this time – a small terracotta bas-relief discovered at Akra in the North-west Frontier Province and two stone statues at Bhumara in Central India. Earlier sculptural evidence, a Buddhist railing at Amaravati and a Sri Lankan Buddhist frieze, can at best be considered circumstantial. In literature too the Vedic references, though now considered part of Ganesha worship, are subject to scholarly doubts. It is only in the eighth century that we get clear mention of the elephant-faced god in the opening stanzas of Bhavabhuti's play, 'Malati-Madhava'.

The Mudgala Purana plays around with a double entry. It lists the official thirty-two forms, sixteen of which are widely accepted. It also provides an interesting variation of eight Ganeshas overcoming eight demons, representing the eight human passions; Ekadanta (single tusk) vanquished Moda (arrogance); Vakratunda (curved-trunk), Matsara (jealousy); Mahodara (big belly), Moha (infatuation); Gajanana (elephant-face), Lobha (greed); Lambodara (flabby belly), Krodha (anger); Vikata (grotesque), Kama (carnal love); Vighnaraja (King of obstacles), Mamata (ego); Dhumravarna (smoke-colour), Abhimana (self-regard).

Apart from a shuffling around and additions to his usual symbols, one notices an infusion, a virtual flooding of colour into the hitherto monochromatic form of Ganesha. Of the thirty-two forms, half are bright red and the others are gold, blue,

Painting by Jogen Chowdhury. Contemporary.

yellow and black. Colour symbolism associated with occult, particularly Tantric practices, begin to add a definite dimension to the meaning of Ganesha. Yellow speaks of the intellect, red of the active, the passionate, the physical; white for purity and nearness to the ultimate perception, which is blue and spiritual. Gold radiates the lustre of divinity and black evokes the darkness of death and destruction. The colours also indicate the *gunas* or qualities that define the natural proclivities of things and people. White, gold and yellow tend to be *sattvik* or pure, red tends to be *rajasik* or active, blue and black tend to be *tamasik*, inertia with its potential for destruction. *Rajas, sattva* and *tamas* also extend to the triad of Creator, Preserver and Destroyer (Brahma, Vishnu and Shiva). Ganesha seems to be appropriating to himself the lineaments of the Trinity, the position to which the Ganapatya sect had elevated him.

Some texts also lay down characteristics for Ganesha images. He should be dwarfish, grotesque, rotund, pot-bellied with hidden ankles, curving trunk, bald elephant-head, flapping ears, tiny eyes, black teeth and a smoke-grey complexion.

The 'Sharada-tilaka-tantra' lists fifty forms based on the ideology of the letters of the Sanskrit alphabet; each letter being a *shakti* and a consort of Ganapati. We need not enter the bewildering jungle of qualities and attributes that these represent. The Ganesha cult was already going into detail that at times verged on religious hair-splitting. It is enough to note that his personality was acquiring subtler shades of meaning.

All this, however, charts out the area of his operations. He uses or manipulates obstacles for all manner of situations which call for all kinds of strategy, including feminine wiles and allurements — which is where the *shakti* or consort enters the scene. As helpmate and companion, she contributes powers like Truth and Effulgence at one end of the spectrum, Coyness and Enchantment at the other.

A close look at some of the thirty-two forms mentioned in the Mudgala Purana will give us a fair idea of Ganapati as he is worshipped today.

*Vighna-Ganapati* (Obstacle-Remover): Burnished gold, bejewelled, ten-armed, carrying conch, sugarcane stalk, flower-arrows, axe, noose, discus, broken tusk, goad, bunch of flowers and reeds. This form seems to have shades of Kama, god of love and Krishna added to his usual personality. He is pleasantly sensuous, alluring, distracting and therefore well-equipped to obstruct.

*Heramba-Ganapati* (Protector of the Weak): White, five-headed form with ten arms, riding a lion. The hands bless and protect using the traditional gestures and hold the noose, the rosary, tusk, goad and *modaka*. The lion links him to his mother, Durga.

*Maha-Ganapati* (Ganapati the Great): A favourite with the tenth century Ganapatya sect which gave Ganesha a great boost. He carries the usual objects, with a difference or two. He holds the many-seeded pomegranate fruit, symbol of fertility and a pot of jewels; and has his consort on his lap in a fond embrace. A variant of this form conveys a rich and heavy opulence, almost hedonistic in its effect.

*Heramba, Orissa pat. Five-headed, white and riding a lion, this is the form which became most popular in Nepal.*

Ganapati sits on a triangle, within a six-petalled lotus spread out on a jewelled throne under a *parijata* tree in Ratnadvipa (Island of Jewels) set in a billowing ocean of sugarcane juice. The tree was stolen by Krishna himself from Indra's garden for his wife Satyabhama. The heady sweetness of this image with the erotic overtones of its tantric 'feminine' triangle, and juice of the sugarcane which is the bow of the god of love, are characteristic of Tantric ritual.

*Nritta-Ganapati* (Dancing Ganapati): Bright yellow and dancing under the *kalpataru* or wish-fulfilling tree. He holds the usual objects but leaves a hand free to trace the dance movements. A form that establishes his links with Shiva as Nataraja, Lord of the Dance.

*Ucchistha-Ganapati* (Ganesha, sexually roused): An openly erotic form. Both he and his consort are nude, though bedecked. The fertility associations are overt and explicit.

*Yoga-Ganapati* (Ganapati in yogic contemplation): Dressed in blue, the colour of spirituality, with his body red like the rising sun, one of his hands has the staff of yoga. A meditating, awesome figure, functioning on a plane half-way to salvation.

It is hard to think of Ganesha as a happily married man with brides chosen in the customary Indian manner by anxious parents. But that was precisely what he was before his two wives, Buddhi (wisdom) and Siddhi (success) were upstaged by his myriad consorts. A charming legend tells of the two brothers arguing over who should get married first. Shiva and Parvati set them a race – whoever went round the world fastest would be the first to marry.

The younger son, Kartikeya, realising there was no time to waste, set off on his peacock. The elder boy, Ganesha, who had no intention of undertaking such a long and arduous journey, and who lived largely by his wits anyway, hit upon a clever stratagem. He sat his parents down, sang their praises, walked round them seven times and declared that he had won the race! When his parents protested, questioning the validity of his claim, he quoted the Vedas and the Shastras to prove that seven circumambulations round his parents by a devoted son equalled one round the whole world! They could not fault him on his knowledge of the sacred texts and went ahead with the wedding preparations.

Kartikeya returned to a cosy domestic scene – Ganesha and two wives who had, by then, borne him two sons – Kshema (welfare) and Labha (profit). Enraged, he returned to a distant mountain retreat, far away from his parents and his brother.

Ganesha has two wives, Buddhi (wisdom) and Siddhi (success); alternately,

Riddhi (increase, prosperity) and Siddhi. Other variant pairs are: Bharati (learning) and Shri (prosperity); Buddhi and Kubuddhi (cunning).

Ganesha is also shown in the *Ashtasiddhi* form with eight consorts who are the eight siddhis (powers or levels) of mental achievement.

In the fifty *shaktis* of Ganesha which are associated with the fifty letters of the Sanskrit alphabet, we have a minutiae of psychological observation. Apart from the recognisable *Shaktis* like Parvati and Lakshmi we have Medha (intelligence), Kanti (lustre), Suyasha (good name and reputation), Nanda (joy), Chanchala (restiveness), Kalaratri (night of destruction). A formidable array of temptations or weapons to let loose on the enemy — obstacles truly come in many forms.

The rampant appearance of innumerable *Shaktis* or female energies coincide with the influence of Tantrism and the growth of the Ganapatya sect which flourished in the tenth century. It set up a parallel phallic cult to the mainstream Shivalinga cult. There seemed almost nothing Ganesha could do that could not be bettered by pairing him with an associate *Shakti*. And unlike his father, whose erotic adventures were almost entirely confined to one mate, Ganesha was frankly polygamous.

*Ganesha in amorous dalliance with his two consorts.*

As Ganesha grew in stature, vying with his father for popularity, we encounter a half-feminine form as a parallel to Shiva-Ardhanariswara. Vainayaki, sometimes referred to as Ganeshani, is male from the neck up and voluptuously female the rest of the way down. Many icons have been found of this form although there is no textual evidence to support it. We do, of course, have a convincing story to lend it plausibility — it was found in a temple inscription. Seeing his father embracing and merging with his mother, Uma to become Ardhanarishwara, Ganesha too did the same with his wife.

It was not strictly a fair division in his case — the male seems to have got hold of the more prestigious end of the human stick, the head. Shiva's distribution of privilege, when he did decide to share it, was more equitable. It was a perfect vertical split. He kept back nothing for the male by way of unfair advantage.

## Symbol

Underlying the names and forms, making the image come alive with meaning, is the symbolism that attaches to it. A symbol is a good way of transcending the material fact, going beyond the face or facade of things to the inner reality. It is a deep-rooted Indian habit, to read meanings into everything, to see or accept nothing as it

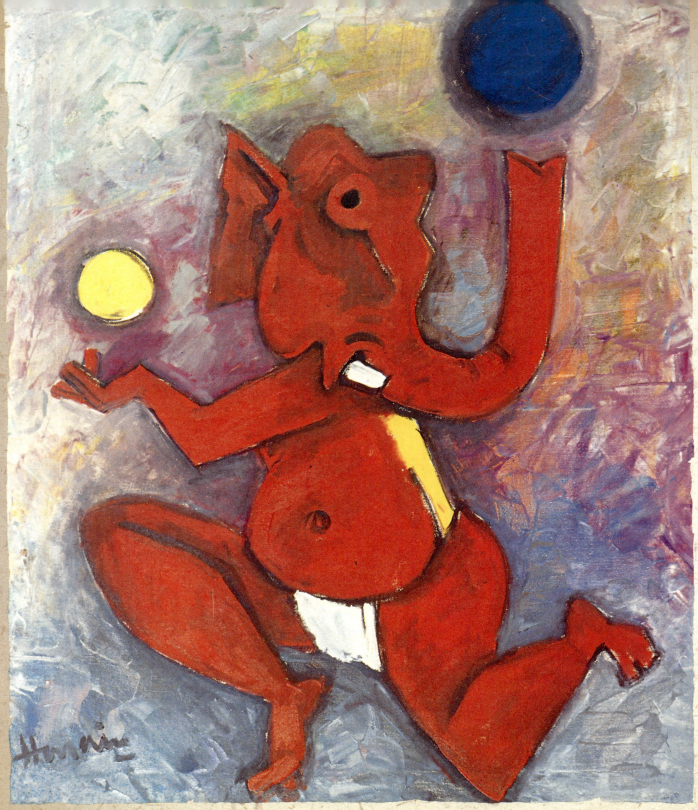
*Painting by M.F. Hussain. Contemporary.*

seems. It is one of the better tricks of the Indian mind, going as far back as the Vedas. The Rig Veda distinguishes between two kinds of truth – *ritham* (reality) and *satyam* (fact) – the first has to do with *manas* (the mind), the second with *vak* (speech).

A symbolic survey of Ganesha would involve scrutinising his physique, the objects he holds in his hands, his gestures, his mount, his stance, the marks on his forehead and, of course, his mates or consorts.

Firstly, his figure. Above is the elephant-head. It stands for the larger and more significant part of him which is the overseeing, eternal witness, the Unmanifest Supreme, the macrocosm. Below, is the manifest, the mortal, the microcosm, represented by the human torso. The etymology underlines this. '*Ga*' stands for *gaja* (elephant) and *na* for *nara* (man). *Gaja* again splits into *ga* for the yogic goal of release into the Unmanifest, and *ja* for the beginning, the source, the resonance of the sacred syllable OM which, periodically and cyclically, sets off the process of creation. As the *pati*, the lord of *ga* and *na*, he is the Lord of all, Manifest and Unmanifest.

He is also referred to as 'Omkaraswarupa' the personification of OM. Ganesha is also supposed to symbolise in his person, the metaphysical concept *tat tvam asi* (you are that) i.e. you (the manifest) are (by your existence) that (the Unmanifest). The Manifest and the Unmanifest are one, and the meeting of them as man and elephant in Ganesha symbolises, and therefore reminds one, of this.

Every deity is represented by a sound or incantation (*mantra*), a sacred diagram (*yantra*) and an icon.

The *mantra* for Ganesha is OM GAN and the *yantra* is a *svastika*. The cross of the *svastika* represents the multiple that arises from the basic unity, the dot. Each branch bends in a curve away from the centre or Truth, moving along the circumference; the way to Truth is not direct.

The single tusk symbolises the numeral one, from which everything starts. Before that there is only *shunya* (zero) or nothing, the Unmanifest. The tusk, in short, is *maya*, the illusory world, the manifest. Therefore it creates and supports the world; the tusk stands for strength and power; indivisibility as opposed to durability and multiplicity. The tusk is also the symbol of a ploughshare, a throwback to Ganesha as Lord of Harvests, his Dravidian past.

Legend tells of how Ganesha lost his other tusk. Parashurama had circled the world twenty-one times exterminating the *kshatriya* (martial) race, avenging the death of his father, Jamadagni. After the massacre, he came to Kailasa to thank Shiva who had provided the weapon, his famous axe. Ganesha stopped him, saying Shiva was conversing with Parvati. Parashurama flew into a rage and hurled his axe at him. Out of respect for his father's weapon, Ganesha did not counter the blow, but took the force of it on his tusk, thereby losing it. It is also said that he broke off his tusk to use it as a stylus for taking down the epic Mahabharata as Vyasa dictated it. According to the Tantric tradition he used it to take down the Tantric texts as Shiva expounded them to Parvati. Yet another legend tells of how he hurled it at the demon Gajasura, turned him into a rat and used him as his mount.

The trunk stands for wisdom and it curls, representing the round-about way to Truth. It can turn to either right or left in its search for Truth. His four arms represent the four Vedas and activate the four elements.

The large, flapping ears are compared to winnowing baskets. As they receive the words of men they blow away the chaff of falsehood, leaving the grains of truth behind. They stand for discrimination and discernment, separating the essential from the non-essential. All experience should be subject to this process. The wise discriminate.

The ear is an important orifice in Indian metaphysics because, of all the sense organs, it is the one that received the *Vedas* or *Shruti* (that which is heard), and the *Vedas* are revealed Truth, the quintessence of knowledge.

Ganesha's great belly is equated with space, vast enough to hold all of wisdom and all of life.

From his person we move to the objects he holds in his hands. The noose snares *moha* (delusion) and the goad is the impeller and driver of the universe. It goads one in the right direction. The *modaka* is wisdom; the many-seeded pomegranate is a phallic symbol, full to bursting with the power of germination. Indeed any fruit he holds stands for both wisdom and life. The rosary stands for prayer: Ganesha is referred to as the cause of prayers, chief among the greatest of them. At times he holds the trident and the axe, his father's insignia, reflecting an aspect of Shiva, just as when he rides the lion, he assumes an aspect of his mother, Durga. The pot of jewels signifies riches and the pot of water, the sanctifying waters of the Ganga, his aunt, who brought him to life after Parvati, her sister, had fashioned him with dirt and earth. His sacred thread and girdle are serpents, reminders of Shiva and an excuse for a legend.

It had been a long and successful day. Offerings had come pouring in. Ganesha had had more than his usual share of

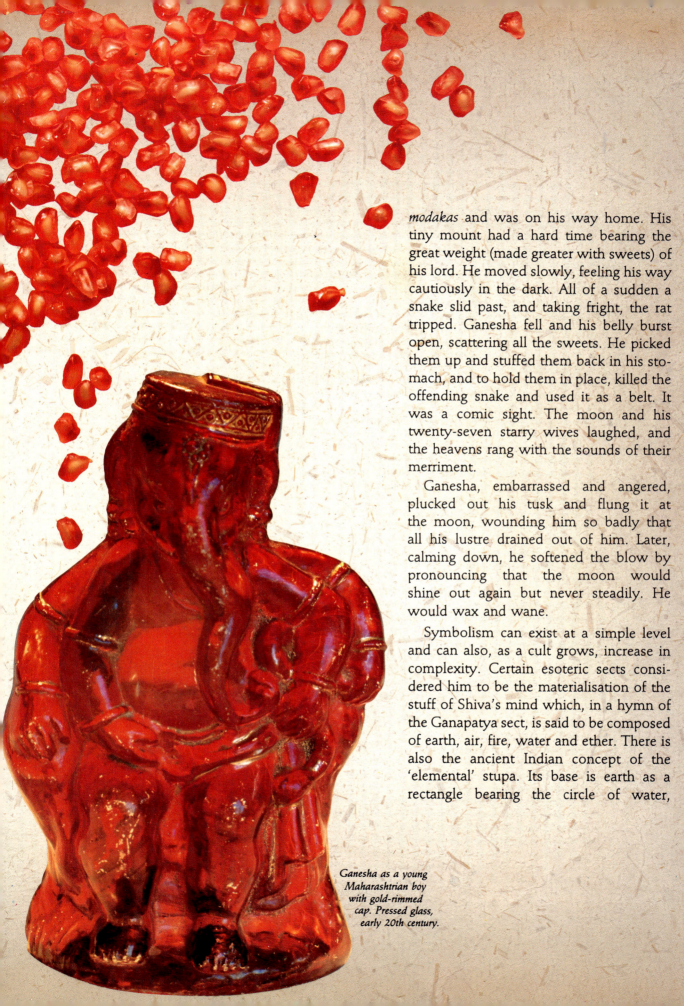

*Ganesha as a young Maharashtrian boy with gold-rimmed cap. Pressed glass, early 20th century.*

*modakas* and was on his way home. His tiny mount had a hard time bearing the great weight (made greater with sweets) of his lord. He moved slowly, feeling his way cautiously in the dark. All of a sudden a snake slid past, and taking fright, the rat tripped. Ganesha fell and his belly burst open, scattering all the sweets. He picked them up and stuffed them back in his stomach, and to hold them in place, killed the offending snake and used it as a belt. It was a comic sight. The moon and his twenty-seven starry wives laughed, and the heavens rang with the sounds of their merriment.

Ganesha, embarrassed and angered, plucked out his tusk and flung it at the moon, wounding him so badly that all his lustre drained out of him. Later, calming down, he softened the blow by pronouncing that the moon would shine out again but never steadily. He would wax and wane.

Symbolism can exist at a simple level and can also, as a cult grows, increase in complexity. Certain esoteric sects considered him to be the materialisation of the stuff of Shiva's mind which, in a hymn of the Ganapatya sect, is said to be composed of earth, air, fire, water and ether. There is also the ancient Indian concept of the 'elemental' stupa. Its base is earth as a rectangle bearing the circle of water,

ascending to the triangle of fire, surmounted by the crescent of air, from the middle of which rises a flame-shaped symbol. Ganesha's seated figure can be made to correspond to this. His plump, crossed legs form the rectangle of earth, his round belly the circle of water, his tusk, mouth and upper trunk taken together the triangle of fire, his *tilaka,* the crescent of air, and his third eye, long, narrow and tapered, the flame of ether. He becomes the *yantra*, the charmed diagram of the ascendant Lord of the elements and therefore of the universe.

Another *yantra* superimposed on his figure is the letter OM to which the lines of his body lend themselves readily. He is considered to be a manifestation of OM.

Ganesha's mount, the rat, deserves special mention. His symbolic journey through Ganesha iconography is eventful. He is a Vedic rat. The Yajur Veda mentions the rat as Shiva's share of animal offering in a ritual — a symbolic mouse was made of dough and buried in the earth. The mouse as the symbol of the Vedic god Agni, was appropriated by Ganapati who was essentially Agni. As part of the earlier solar myth, the mouse stands for the darkness of the bowels of the earth into which he burrows, avoiding light. The rat also is associated with the depredation of fields at harvest time and therefore needed to be overcome or ridden by the Lord of Harvests, one of Ganesha's early aspects.

The rat too merits a story and a lineage. The sage Vamadeva cursed a Gandharva, an aerial being, and turned him into a rat. The chattering, restless mouse disturbed another great sage, Parashara. He appealed to Ganesha who caught the mouse and used him as his vehicle.

In the popular imagination the rat is swift, stealthy and destructive; he can chew his way through anything, squeeze through the smallest hole. He was therefore a good choice for the lord in charge of obstacles who had to be everywhere and anywhere at short notice.

The elephant as a symbol was a good acquisition for Ganesha. The stampeding elephant must have been the terror of the farmer and therefore needed to be appeased by worship. The memory of an elephant is proverbial. Gentle and harmless, he uses his great strength only when provoked. He moves gracefully and ceremonially and is equally at home in forest or temple. In the Jataka Tales the Buddha, in his previous births, took the form of an elephant many times. Classical literature is full of references to beautiful women with rounded hips, moving with the grace of an elephant. The elephant, King of the Indian jungle, makes a good head for the lord of wisdom and learning.

OM GANESHAYA NAMAH

अव पश्यातात् । अव पुरस्तात् अवोत्तरत्तात् ।
अव दक्षिणात्तात् । अवचोर्ध्वातात् । अवाधरत्तात्
सर्वता मां पाहि पाहि समंतात् ।

*Close me in, surround me, Lord*
*Enclose me quite and shelter me*
*North and south, above, below*
*Before, behind and all around*
*In every way, at every turn*
*Protect me, Lord. Protect me, Lord.*
*Protect me, Lord.*

— *Atharva Veda*

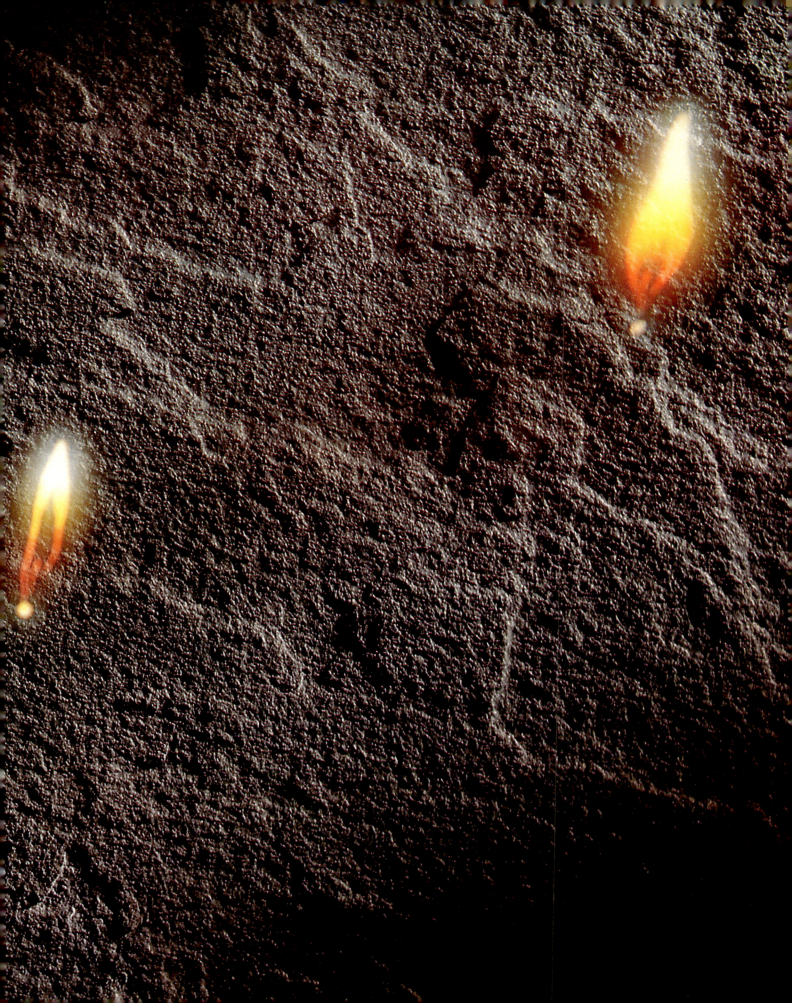

*Durga with Ganesha. The waterpot in the foreground drips water on to the Shivalinga beneath.*

A god is worshipped in a particular form, addressed by a particular name or names and for a particular purpose. He has a general function to perform as well as an immediate petition to grant.

Ganesha is chiefly a remover of obstacles on the path to success but he has other roles to perform and consequently takes on other aspects. He is guardian and protector, and also a god in charge of wisdom and learning.

He started off as guardian and protector of field, crop and harvest, protecting them from stampeding elephants and thieving field mice. These were the obstacles he removed from the path of the farmer, the obstacles that stood in the way of his success and achievement.

He also stood guard, literally; first at his mother's door, protecting her from his father's intrusions, obstructing and barring his way. He guarded monasteries in Nepal, temple entrances in Tibet and stood at remote, dangerous spots in Indonesia, protecting unwary travellers.

There is an ancient Tibetan legend which tells of a doorkeeper who died and was reborn as a demon. He begged the people to put up a memorial statue to him as a *yaksha* and to hang a bell round his neck which he could ring to warn them of

Painting by Manjit Bawa. Contemporary

Varahi: One of the Saptmatrikas

approaching danger. The earliest statues discovered in India of Ganesha show him wearing bells, and art historians feel that this points to his early role as guardian.

Guarding involved protection from disease too, both of mind and body. This explains his association with the Saptamatrikas (seven mothers) with whom he is often seen in early temple sculpture. As protector, guarding people against the malevolent and the malefic, he is also associated with the nine planets, the Navagrahas. The Saptamatrika concept has shades of the mother as protector of the child but with a twist – and this is where Ganesha, standing right next to them, comes in. He is prayed to first, so that children can be saved from the dangers that these goddesses would otherwise threaten them with, for they are essentially malefic, with the power to destroy through prevention. They were born to prevent, as the following story of their genesis demonstrates.

Shiva was fighting the fierce demon Andhakasura, and found that from every drop of blood that fell from the wounded demon, a new demon sprang up. Breathing fire, he created from the flames a *shakti*, Yogeswari. Seven other gods did likewise and so we have the corresponding Saptamatrikas: Brahmani, Maheshwari, Kaumari, Vaishnavi, Varahi, Indrani and Chamundi. These seven, led by Yogeswari, caught each drop of blood as it fell and Andhakasura was finally overcome. Their role was prevention.

They were also looked upon as personifications of the seven harmful mental qualities – pride, anger, illusion, covetousness, envy, fault-finding and talebearing, with their leader, Yogeswari, representing Kama, desire. Appeasing the Saptamatrikas through Ganesha would mean freedom from negative emotions and characteristics.

Ganesha was also worshipped as the deity who could intercede on behalf of the devotees with the Navagrahas who, through their configurations and movements, controlled the destinies of people. They were usually worshipped collectively in order to ensure that none of them, even for a moment, felt neglected.

*Ganesha holding up the Mahabharata.*

Somewhere along the way, guarding and protecting, Ganesha assumed the aspects of wisdom and learning. He appears in two separate legends as a scribe. Vyasa, author of the Mahabharata, needed an extraordinary scribe, one who could write as fast as Vyasa could think. Ganesha offered his services and sat down to write, using his own tusk as the stylus. But he too had his conditions: Vyasa could not stop to think. His words had to flow continuously, without a break. In the Tantric tradition, he appears again as a very

special scribe; as Shiva expounded the Tantras to Parvati, he recorded them.

There is some difference of opinion on how Ganesha got associated with the written word. P.C. Bagchi suggests that it is the result of confusion about the word *siddhi*. The alphabet was called *siddham* and enumeration of the alphabet began with the word *siddhi*. As Siddhidata, he got linked to the letter, therefore with words and learning, and ultimately to wisdom. Bhandarkar says it is mistaken identification of him with the Vedic god of wisdom, and Gopinath Rao, the iconographist, says he was identified with the celestial guru, Brihaspati. A Vedic hymn refers to him as Brihaspati and Brahmanaspati. Brahmanaspati, lord of prayer and meditation, and Brihaspati, teacher of the gods would, between them, cover wisdom and learning.

Ananda Coomaraswamy says that *gana* stands for 'early lists or collections of related works' – the association with writing and record-keeping is obvious. Ganesha wrote down the epic Mahabharata, the essence of Indian experience. He also recorded and preserved the Tantras, repositories of occult and mystic experiments and experience, hidden and esoteric. This would explain how he assumed the mantle of learning.

Ganesha's primary function was to act as Remover of Obstacles on the road to success. This extended to his role as guardian, protector and preventer. He also assumed, through a quirk of divine fate,

the aspects of learning and wisdom. As an elephant-god, he turned out to be a good load-bearer.

## Worship at home

The worship of any deity involves getting the worship corner ready to receive the god or goddess, the invitation, the seating, bathing, dressing, decoration, offerings of worship with incense, flowers and light, offerings of food which later the worshipper consumes as *prasadam*, blessed and sanctified with the deity's pleasure. With salutation and circumambulation the *puja* or worship is concluded. All this is laid down in sixteen orderly steps.

Ganesha is given the same treatment except that the offerings and some prayers differ. He is invited specifically: 'O Lord of the World, Lord of lords, radiating lustre, step in, Gananayaka, and accept my worship. my offerings, to you.' Then substituting with verbal description whatever cannot actually be offered, the *puja* begins. He is seated on a golden throne set with jewels. He is offered a sip of the sacred waters of the world, his feet washed with the same; then he is bathed with the five nectars (*panchamrutham*) – milk, curd, ghee, honey and jaggery – cleansing him with fresh water between 'nectars'. Each of these, being the best of its type, has to be equated with a legendary standard of excellence and this is stated: the milk is the milk of Kamadhenu, the wish-fulfilling heavenly cow; the curd partakes of the lustre of the moon – white, smooth and cool; the ghee is the food of the gods themselves with a long Vedic past; the honey, extract of all herbs, is the essence of good health, the elixir of life with herbal healing powers; and jaggery. extract of sugarcane, the epitome of sweetness.

Ganesha is now given a red garment and the sacred thread, saying it is silver. He is smeared with red sandal paste and offered red or yellow flowers. The lamp is lit, bells chime and the food is offered in six symbolic mouthfuls – not to his body,

but to his five vital breaths (*panchaprana*) and the One beyond – Brahman, the Absolute. The *puja* ends, asking not for any specific worldly need, but for 'a firm and steady devotion' so that he could guide the devotee to 'the path of salvation'. Then the circumambulation (*pradakshina*) is performed by turning around in one spot, saying 'whatever sins I have gathered through my life, may this circumambulation destroy'. Addressing him as destroyer of the pride of Gajasura and evil aerial spirits, the final prayer is said, giving him the honorific 'Lord of Obstacles and best among gurus'.

The worship ends with an apology, beautifully worded: 'I am ignorant of the gracious ways of invitation, welcome or entertainment. You, my Lord, will have to perfect it for me.'

Ganesh Chaturthi is a festival that starts on the fourth day of the bright half of the month of Bhadrapada which is around August-September. It can be celebrated for two, five, seven or eleven days.

The day commemorates certain events connected with Ganesha. It is the day on which he materialised as Mayureshwara, to kill the demon Sindhu who had acquired extraordinary powers through the worship of Surya. Mayureshwara is also one of the Ashtavinayakas, a group of eight naturally formed (*swayambhu*) Ganeshas in Maharashtra. They are important pilgrim sites. Also, this is the birth that Shiva has chosen to celebrate in Kailasa.

On Ganesh Chaturthi day, the *puja* is different only in that the idol, a clay one, has to be first installed and then immersed at the end of the festival. A *puja* is performed twice everyday, once in the morning and again in the evening. He is offered special leaves and flowers, twenty-one of each, and white *durva* grass. The idol is formally installed and given life in the presence of Brahma, Vishnu and Shiva, and the Vedas. Touching him with blades of *durva* grass, he is brought to life step by step, and made to go through the fifteen rites of passage that each Hindu goes through in his lifetime. The sixteenth which is for death is omitted.

Then, as usual, the Ganesha mantra is chanted, and a Ganesha prayer. The last *puja* done, the family gathers round. Rice

grains are placed on his head and the idol is moved, symbolically unseating him. Humbly requested to return next year, he is immersed. Ganesha has been consigned to the elements.

In Maharashtra, in Bombay and Poona especially, the *visarjana* or immersion is also a public, community event. It was Lokmanya Tilak who, in 1892, made Ganesh Chaturthi a mass celebration. He did it in order to increase national awareness as part of the Independence movement. Neighbourhood Ganeshas are worshipped and brought to immersion sites where huge crowds gather to bid him an emotional and frenzied farewell. In Bombay, as the sun sets over a darkening sea, the images are taken out in boats, and as each one is immersed, a cry is raised asking him to return. Emotion wells up in repeated waves of sound, full-throated and devout. It is a mammoth public send-off to their beloved god as *parthiva* (of the earth). He is returning to it only to rise again the following year.

## Temple worship

An ancient text, Rupamandana, lays down the general rules for building a Ganesha temple with positions for his wives, his mother, Kubera, Saraswati and four gatekeepers. But the most sacred Ganesha temples are the *swayambhu* (self-generated) sites. Ganesha is supposed to have manifested himself at these sites in natural forms, usually rocks. The form is daubed with red and a legend, rather than a temple, grows round it. The Ashtavinayakas (eight Vinayakas) of Maharashtra are a good example. These are visited in a laid-down sequence and their names are always taken in Maharashtrian wedding ceremonies.

*Moreshwar* (Lord of the Peacock) at Morgaon. It is the foundation of the Ganapatya sect. The village was once full of peacocks and is itself peacock-shaped. The legend is of Sindhu, son of King Chakrapani, who through worship of Surya became powerful and arrogant. Attacking and conquering the gods, he imprisoned them in his city, Gandaki. Ganesha, born as Mayureshwara, or Moreshwar, riding a peacock, liberated the gods on Ganesh Chaturthi day, cutting Sindhu into three parts. Morgaon is supposed to be situated at the spot where the head fell. The idol is a rock, facing north.

*Ballaleswar* (Lord of Ballala) at Pali. Ballala was the son of a merchant named Kalyan and his wife Indumati. The child was an ardent Ganesha worshipper and soon had all his friends following him to the forest. The parents of the boys complained to Kalyan who, angered that his son was idling away his days and corrupting the village boys, beat him severely, threw away the Ganesha idol, tied him up and abandoned him, saying, 'Let Ganesha free you'. The boy prayed to him, Ganesha appeared and freed him, and then disappeared into the rock, which is the *swayambhu* idol at Ballaleswar. It faces East. Behind it is the Dhundi Vinayaka temple which one visits first, because it is supposed to have the idol that Ballala's father threw away.

*Siddhi Vinayaka* (Vinayaka as success) at Siddhatek is situated on the banks of the Bhima river. The legend about this temple talks of the success of Vishnu himself as a result of praying to Ganesha.

Brahma once thought of creating a world with Ganesha's blessings. As he did so, Vishnu woke up and from his ears two fierce demons, Madhu and Kaitaba, emerged. Vishnu fought them for 5000 years with no success. Shiva pointed out that he had started without worshipping Ganesha. So Vishnu invoked him on the hill of Siddhatek, destroyed the demons successfully and consecrated the spot.

*Chintamani* (Jewel of the Mind) at Thevoor. King Abhijit and Queen Gunavati had a son, Gana who once visited the sage Kapila. Gana coveted the *chintamani* (wish-fulfilling stone) that Kapila used when entertaining him. Kapila refused to part with it, but Gana took it forcibly. The sage was then advised by Durga to worship Ganesha. With the powers he got through that worship, Kapila fought and killed Gana. Abhijit returned the jewel to Kapila who by then had ceased to want it. Ganesha then called himself Chintamani and stayed on at the spot under a *kadamba* tree after which the village was named Kadambanagar. There is a lake here called Chintamani Sarovar. Indra is supposed to have performed penance here. Brahma too steadied his mind with penance at this spot, hence it is called Thevoor, derived from *sthavara* (steady). The image is of the head and trunk alone.

*Girijatmaka* (son of Girija) at Lenyadri. This *swayambhu* is situated on the banks of the Kukdi river. It is at a height and has Buddhist rock-cut carvings.

Parvati, wanting a son, prayed to Ganesha for twelve years. Ganesha, pleased with her devotion, was born as her child. The rock faces south and is specially sacred because Ganesha's thread ceremony was performed here.

*Varada Vinayaka* (Vinayaka as Blesser) at Mahad. Rukmangada, son of a brave, generous king, became a leper for no fault of his own. A sage's wife was attracted to him and because he repelled her advances, she cursed him. Rukmangada went to Kadambanagar, bathed in the Chintamani lake and was cured. Hearing of the sage's wife and her desire for Rukmangada, Indra assumed his form and had a son by her, Gritsamada. He later became the author of a Rig Vedic Mandala. Mocked by his companions, he got to know of his mother's infidelity and cursed her; then to cleanse himself of the sin of cursing his mother, he came to Mahad and was blessed by Vinayaka. Gritsamada was also the founder of the Ganapatya sect, according to their tradition.

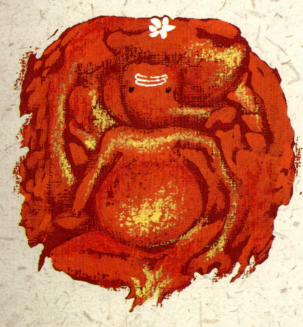

*Vighneshwara* (Lord of Obstacles) at Ozar. King Abhinandana performed many sacrifices in order to become a second Indra. Indra, hearing of it, sent Kala himself (Time as Destroyer), in the form of Vighnasura to obstruct the sacrifices. All other Vedic rites also came to a halt and the world suffered as a consequence. The gods worshipped Ganesha who conquered Vighnasura and made him one of his *ganas*. Vighna begged that Ganesha would use his name as a prefix and also that he would stay on at Ozar. Ganesha agreed.

*Mahaganapati* (Ganapati the Great) at Ranjangaon. Ranjangaon was established by Shiva himself as Manipur. The legend has to do with Gritsamada, a devotee of Ganesha. He sneezed and a child, Tripurasura, emerged from his nostrils, and he treated him as his own son. Tripurasura went on to conquer all three worlds by worshipping Ganesha with Vedic mantras. He became King of three cities made of gold, silver and iron. Ganesha prophesied that none but Shiva could destroy him or his cities, and that he would do so with a single arrow. The gods went to Shiva who set out to fight Tripurasura. He did not succeed at first. It was Narada who told him he should have worshipped Ganesha before he started the battle and gave him the appropriate prayer. Shiva succeeded and in gratitude established Ganesha there as Mahaganapati.

Worship has to do with ritual — daily, occasional, home or temple. Legends cling to idol and site or even objects of worship to become a treasure-hoard of stories. It is futile to ask if they are true or false — they have the truth of all mythology, the truth of human vision, faith and devotion.

The *shami* leaf is one of the twenty-one leaves offered to Ganesha during the *Chaturthi puja*. There is a story about how it came to be part of Ganesha worship.

In the city of Vitihotra, there lived a brahmin Aurava and his wife, Sumedha. They had a daughter Shamika who, in time, married Mandara, son of the great sage, Dhaumya.

One day, the sage Bhrishundi, a devotee of Ganesha, visited Dhaumya's ashram and was received with the customary rites of hospitality by the young daughter-in-law, Shamika. He was given water to wash his feet and offered fruits and roots to eat.

All was going well and smoothly when the mishap occurred. Bhrishundi was a man with an unusual appearance. He had an elephant's head, just like his favourite god. The young Shamika could not restrain herself for long. She burst out laughing at the strange sight of a human being sitting down to a meal, head bent, trunk swaying over his plate of fruits and roots.

The inevitable happened. The angry sage cursed Shamika, turning her into a tree under which no one would want to take shelter; a tree, moreover, full of thorns, the *shami* tree.

Aurava, hearing of the unfortunate incident, began to worship Ganesha. He did so for twelve years. Ganesha appeared and explained that since Bhrishundi was an ardent devotee of his, he could not wipe out the effects of the curse totally. He could, however, modify it and bring some joy into the young girl's life. She would, henceforth, be a blessed, and not a cursed tree. He ordained that worship of him with the *shami* leaf would meet with certain success.

*Durva* grass is used in all *pujas* but is a special favourite with Ganesha. There is more than one story to explain not only its greatness and efficacy, but its associations with Ganesha.

Once there lived a *kshatriya* named Sulabha and his wife, Sumudra. One day, while listening to a recital of the Puranas, a poor brahmin mendicant, Madhusudana, arrived and joined the gathering. Sulabha, in his arrogance, laughed at him – he did, indeed, cut a sorry figure in that crowd of prosperous citizens. Feeling insulted and humiliated, Madhusudana cursed Sulabha, turning him into a bull. Sumudra retaliated by cursing Madhusudana, who turned into an ass. As a parting thrust, the mendicant, while turning into an ass, cursed Sumudra, turning her into a *chandali*, a woman of lowly caste.

One day, the *chandali* was caught in a heavy shower of rain. She tried to take shelter in nearby Ganesha temple, but the worshippers chased her away. She found a patch of dry *durva* grass, and plucking some of it, lit a fire to warm herself. While blowing on it, a single blade flew up and away, right into the inner sanctum of the temple, came to rest on Ganesha's head, and lay there while the *puja* was in progress. In the meantime, the bull and the ass also turned up and started grazing on the patch of *durva*, only to be driven away by the *chandali*. In the scuffle that followed, more *durva* flew up and rested on Ganesha's trunk and feet – the grass, so to say, was getting holier by the minute!

The persistent *chandali* entered the temple unseen and started eating the sanctified offerings that were handed around. She was spotted again, and not only chased out, but also beaten up. But this time, she had a divine protector, Ganesha himself, pleased with all the *durva* that had come to rest on his holy person. He saved not only her, but the other two, restoring them to their normal human forms.

Kaundinya, a devotee of Ganesha in the city of Sthavara told his wife, Ashraya the following story when she asked him why Ganesha was made to bear such a heavy load of *durva* on his head. She wanted to know why so many *durva* blades were being offered to him.

In the court of Yama, the dread god of death, the heavenly nymph, Tilottama, danced, exciting Yama himself. Impassioned by the sight of her, he shed his semen and of that seed, a fiery demon, Anala, was born, striking terror into the hearts of the assembled gods.

They fell to praying, invoking Ganesha, who appeared as a child and growing enormous, instantly swallowed up the offending demon. The god soon began to feel the effects of the fire raging in his belly. He also began to fear that it would consume the entire world. Anala had to be extinguished, exterminated.

The gods tried their best – Indra with the cool rays of the moon, Vishnu with the soothing petals of his divine lotus, Varuna with all his waters. Shiva even sent a many-hooded serpent to lick him up. It 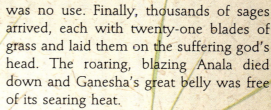 was no use. Finally, thousands of sages arrived, each with twenty-one blades of grass and laid them on the suffering god's head. The roaring, blazing Anala died down and Ganesha's great belly was free of its searing heat.

Kaundinya decided to demonstrate the powers of *durva* to Ashraya beyond all doubt. He handed her a blade of *durva* grass and asked her to go to Indra and bring him back an equivalent weight in gold. Indra sent her to Kubera, the god of wealth. To Kubera's utter astonishment, all his wealth, even his whole city could not outweigh that single blade of *durva* grass.

It is thus, with the magic of story, that Indian faith sustains itself. The stories are funny and serious at the same time; convoluted, absurd and intriguing; in short, all that legend should be to become part of a living culture.

History, legend and myth in India have always mingled making both sense and nonsense of one another – what remains is the story which has its own innate truth and meaning. These are extracted by narrator and listener alike through the mere act of telling and listening, and constitute the living truth of a collective cultural experience. It is not an oversimplification to say that when a myth dies, some bit of its culture dies with it.

त्वमेव सर्व खलु इदं ब्रह्मासि।
त्वं ज्ञानमयो विज्ञानमयोऽभि।

The reach of knowledge, all its ways
The facts of knowledge, and beyond
The truth of knowledge, and beyond
Truth perceived at journey's end
That all indeed is Brahman here
All this you are, and that we know.
— Atharva Veda

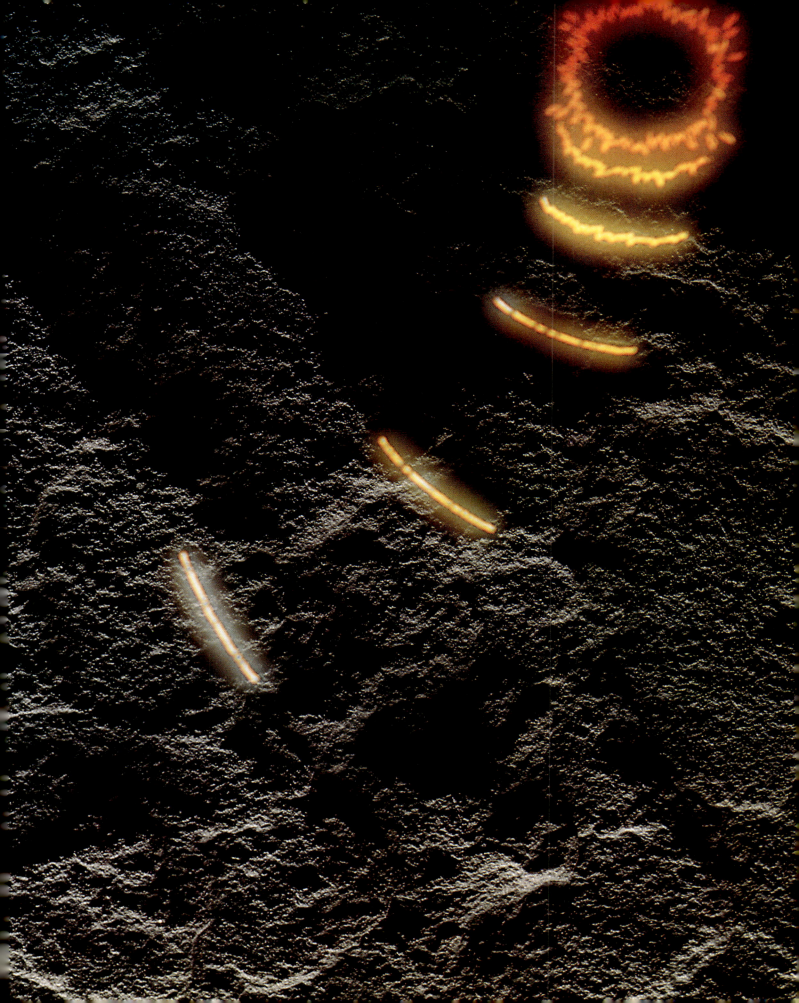

The Ganesha form proliferated, spreading out from its simple field, forest and solar associations to take in the vast expanse of Indian introspection. As the outward manifestation of an increasingly inward journey, there seemed to be no end to the symbolic extensions that this form could absorb. This continued to be the case when he came into contact with Buddhism and when he travelled to other Asian countries like Nepal, Tibet, Burma, Thailand, Indonesia, Indo-China and as far east as China and Japan. Adaptation was a way of life with the Indian gods and the history of Ganesha, both at home and abroad, demonstrates this. On alien soil, he changed aspects and functions and generally integrated with ease. He suffered setbacks in status and stature like any other immigrant. He gave up godhood as he knew it, transforming and even mutating, but never beyond recognition. He kept his form, for one thing, and retained most of his symbols.

Ganesha as Siddhidata (bestower of success) was popular with the Buddhists. Buddhist tradition makes the Buddha himself reveal the mystic *Ganapati-hridaya mantra* to his disciple, Ananda. This *mantra*, like the Gayatri, was personified and given a feminine form, and was perhaps

*One of the oldest forms to be found on alien soil.*

intended to be a *shakti* of Ganesha. In a fragment of sculpture at Sarnath, near Varanasi, he is seen on his mount, in a group of Hindu deities, near the dying Buddha. He is still Hindu and not part of the Buddhist pantheon, but very definitely part of Buddhist mythology. In Bengal there are images of a demon Vinayaka, subdued and conquered by Buddhist goddesses but never banished. Sculpture shows him subordinate and even underfoot but still present as a force to contend with. He was a survivor.

## The Journey north - Nepal, Chinese Turkestan, Tibet

Ganesha had also begun to travel by the early centuries of the Christian era, perhaps even earlier. In Nepal he leads a double and parallel life – Hindu and Buddhist, god and guardian spirit. The ups and downs of his career are largely tied up with sibling rivalry. They reflect the tensions that developed between the sister religions, Buddhism and Hinduism. Interestingly, Nepalese Buddhist mythology responded by creating a rival, Vighnantaka, to keep his Indian counterpart in check. We have the story of a pious Buddhist, a learned man who sat on the banks of the Bagmati river, meditating and performing rites to attain a certain stage of spiritual perfection. Ganesha kept throwing obstacles in his path, obstructing his progress and delaying it. In despair, blocked and prevented at every turn, the harassed man, through the power of meditation, invoked Vighnantaka who materialised, fierce and determined, flashing his third eye, bearing sword and buckler, skull and chopper (Tantric symbols) as well as the familiar *modaka*. Ganesha goes down, still crowned, his hand extended in the *abhaya mudra* (gesture of protection). The Buddhist Vighnantaka triumphs, but the victory seems only partial.

Legend has it that Ganesha worship came to Nepal with the Mauryan Emperor Ashoka's daughter who dedicated a temple to him. There is, in fact, such a temple with inscriptions dating from the eighth to the tenth century, but the actual date of the foundation of the temple is not known. Certainly by the tenth century, amongst both Hindus and Buddhists, Ganesha was firmly lodged as Vinayaka, Remover of Obstacles. This also ties up with the progress of the Ganapatya movement, which peaked at around this time, with its elaborate iconography and dogma.

The Nepalese Ganesha generated his own unique mythology. He was born and brought up differently. Both the Hindu and Buddhist forms had single, simple births partaking of vision and light – a far cry from the welter of conceptions, some of them far from immaculate, that launched his Indian nativity. The Buddhists believe that he manifested himself to a mythical King, Vikramajita, blessing him with much worldly wealth. According to the Hindus, he revealed himself in a ray of sunshine as Surya-Vinayaka. He was born of neither Shiva nor Parvati, but of his own free will to be.

Ganesha has two major forms in Nepal – the Nritta-Ganapati, a dancing form and Heramba-Ganapati, protector of the weak. As Nritta-Ganapati he is shown dancing on his rat who holds a *chintamani* in his mouth. The symbols are Tantric: the god is red and wears a garland of *chintamanis*. The *chintamani*, literally 'jewel of the mind', stands for the enlightened mind or consciousness, the goal of all seekers, and is much used in Tibetan mysticism. It is the philosopher's stone, transforming the finite into the infinite, *samsara* or *karma* into *nirvana*, salvation. In Hinduism too, the *chintamani* is the stone of wish-fulfillment, the ultimate wish being the desire for release.

Heramba, protector of the weak, was by far the most popular form with Hindus and Buddhists alike – five-headed, ten or twelve-armed, riding a lion and generally seen with his *shakti*. In painting, he is given the Mahayana colours. The central head and figure is all white. The heads to the right and left are blue and yellow respectively, the head immediately above the central one, green and the topmost one, red.

The dancing Ganesha is also shown in painting as one of five, each of a different colour. This is probably a Mahayanist assemblage for they grouped their gods in fives and also coloured each differently.

These are the more imposing and dramatic forms. He functions on a more mundane level as a *dvarapala* (gate-keeper), standing guard at the entrance to Buddhist monasteries. In this aspect his companion-guard is Mahakala, a Tibetan import. As a *dvarapala* he may not have had the status of a divinity but the job carried great responsibility with it. In fact, in Tibet, Ganesha was not considerd trustworthy enough for it; he only kept watch over temple entry: he was a mere sentry.

In Nepal, Shiva and Parvati play no part

*Japanese Kangi-ten form. At his initiation ceremony, Ganesha became one with the Universal Spirit manifest in the feminine form of Adi-Buddha Vairochana.*

**Kangi-ten.**
*A Japanese form in which the Soul of the Universe (Male) merges with its Primordial Essence (Female).*

in his simple and visionary manifestations or births, but the iconography retains strong links with both, and that too in the major, popular forms. As Nritta-Ganapati he dances in the shadow of his father, sporting his dread third eye and *tilaka*. As Heramba, protector of the weak, he rides the lion of Durga, his mother, who also protects the weak by destroying evildoers.

In Chinese Turkestan, painted wooden panels discovered near a stupa, as well as frescos in certain cave temples, help us piece together the Ganesha story. He is presented in the traditional Indian form but is also shown wearing a tiger-skin garment over tight-fitting, dark *paijamas* (trousers). It is useful to recall here that the Indian iconographic code allows for local variations in dress and ornamentation; in fact, encourages it. Varahamihira, in Brihatsamhita, says that an idol that is dressed, decorated and ornamented following local customs will turn out to be auspicious, increasing one's prosperity.

There is a fairly rigid code laid down for the 'essential' form but decorative features are excluded from this regimen. As we go farther East, his *vastra* (garment) and *alankara* (adornment) also change. In Cambodia it is a pleated skirt, in Indonesia we could have scarves flowing from a belt, in Thailand a tapering, pointed hairstyle and crown, and so on.

Tibet received him not as a god to be worshipped, but as a guardian at temple entrances, warding off evil spirits. He is not even a guardian of monastic treasures, as in Nepal. In Tibet proper, he is denied even this status. As the demon Vinayaka, he is trodden underfoot by Mahakala who was his fellow door-keeper and equal in Nepal. As a *dharmapala* (keeper of the faith) in Buddhist tradition, Mahakala is repressing the demon-threat of the Hindu faith. In an even more positive portrayal of defeat, Mahakala crushes a Ganapati under each foot — one male, and the other, female. Symbolically, defeating Ganesha along with his *shatki* must have represented a more complete victory.

Nepal too has Ganesha representing the enemy Faith but rarely is the image so wholly hostile. The goddess keeps him underfoot but is not a picture of roused fury, intent on annihilation. He seems to be a feared, but respected, foe.

Apart from being trampled on by Mahakala, he is also overcome by the Tibetan god of wisdom, Manjushri in his Tantric form — fierce, three-eyed, wearing serpent bracelets and anklets, and with a serpent thrown across his breast.

All in all, he had an embattled existence in Tibet. Perhaps, proximity to the source religion posed a real threat. He was too close for comfort. Ganesha, lord of obstacles, wisdom and success had to be divested of his portfolio, and seen to be defeated. The irony is that Mahakala resembles Shiva closely in form and concept, and Manjushri is an alter-ego of Ganesha as lord of wisdom, magnified to Shiva-proportions with his third eye and serpent accessories.

Ganesha's sojourn in Tibet is not all cloud. A Mongolian legend holds out a silver lining. It was the Tibetan saint and missionary, P'ags-pa, who spread the word of Mahayana Buddhism in Mongolia in the thirteenth century. And he did this by making use of Mahakala as a manifestation of Shiva. As his son, Ganesha enjoyed some reflected glory. P'ags-pa's father prayed to Ganesha before the child's birth. Ganesha appeared, put him on his trunk and took him to the top of Mount Meru. From the commanding height of the axis of the world, Ganesha prophesied, pointing towards Mongolia, 'Your son shall conquer this whole country'. P'ags-pa's victory was, in a way, Ganesha's. In a country that had given him reluctant entry, followed by fairly rough treatment, he was at last the power behind an important scene — the spread of Buddhism.

## Southeast Asia

The Indianisation of Indo-China began with Hindu immigration. Worship of Indi-

93

an gods, both Hindu and Buddhist, soon followed. Burma entered the picture because traders came through and to Burma, particularly lower Burma. With these traders were large numbers of Ganesha icons, brought along for protection and success. By the seventh century A.D., Ganesha was worshipped as Mahapienne in Burma though he was kept firmly out of Buddhist temples, except in Mahayanist Upper Burma, where he was given the usual guardian status.

In Indo-China, Shaivism was well established and there was receptivity to the idea of Ganesha, though he never developed into a cult figure or overtook his father. He was popular as prah Kenes, and ceased to be just a guardian and became a scribe, stylus in hand – either Ganesha, scribe of the Mahabharata or Ganesha, scribe of the Tantras dictated by Shiva. The first would be the result of contact with the Indianised Mons of Burma whom they conquered in Thailand, and the second would have come from the Shaivite connection.

Thailand had been occupied by the Mons from Burma and also had Indian travellers and settlers. They Indianised willingly and rapidly. Ganesha inevitably followed with no wide variation, except in dress and style. Unlike Burma, Thailand and Indo-China produced distinctive and highly developed styles of statuary, blending Hindu and Buddhist features with innovative local ornamentation and detailing.

Indonesia was Shaivite too and ready to receive Ganesha. In Java, with his skull ornamentation, third eye and squat thick-set figure, he kept close to Shiva as Bhairava, pot-bellied and fierce. He was found in isolated spots – river crossings and steep slopes. He might therefore have been worshipped by travellers as Remover of Obstacles on difficult and dangerous journeys. In Bali, he was an indoor guardian, standing in temple niches to ward off evil spirits. He looked distinctly Chinese, reflecting the influence of the Chinese settlers who had come to Bali as early as the Hindus. There is sculptural indication to show that Ganesha helped royalty cross over from life into death, easing their journey.

The over-all image of Ganesha in Southeast Asia is tied up with Shiva. The iconography is a rich blend of Hindu and Buddhist styles and concepts, and definitely begins to take on local colour and form. He is guardian, scribe and protector. He never gave rise to a cult but became a familiar, comfortable presence, not always quite a god, but divine enough to serve common human needs.

## the far-eastern sector

In China and Japan, we have a Vinayaka who approximates to the usual Obstacle Remover. In China, where he appeared much earlier, he does so as 'Spirit King of the Elephants', featured in an inscribed stone bas-relief. The inscription dates him clearly – 531 A.D. He is shown with nine other deities, nature and forest spirits, all 'spirit kings'. This indicates his stature. He bears a lotus in his right hand and a *chintamani* in his left. Since the elephant was unknown to China, he was definitely derived from an Indian model, either seen or brought back by one of the many travellers who went in search of Buddhist texts and teachers.

In Japan, he is much more in control, being given the epithet Vajra-Vinayaka and shown holding the *vajra* or sceptre, though still a minor deity. The more important form, both in China and in Japan, was the unusual double form, almost impossible to explain in totality. This is partly because the cult was secret and erotic; and from China, where it originated, there is no example available.

The Japanese form shows two elephants fully robed with arms interlocked and trunks draped over each other's shoulders in a close and graceful elephantine embrace. It is called Kuan-shi-t'ien

in China and Kangi-ten in Japan and is a conglomerate of many ideas and concepts that arose out of Tantric Buddhism. Shakti-worship, Tibetan Yab-yum (father-mother) – the explicit representation of the Mystic Union – and the mystic yogic *mandalas* of Mahayana Buddhism, all contributed to this strange manifestation of Ganesha. The final crystallisation of this cult is attributed to Kobo Daishi. He acquired the knowledge of Kangi-ten through many years of travel and study and drew dramatic attention to it in the ninth century by performing two miracles. When his initiation ceremony was taking place he became One, for an instant, with the Adi-Buddha Vairochana, the Universal Spirit. It was a practical demonstration of Kangi-ten. Again in the presence of the King, while expounding the tenets of his sect, he took on the aspect, for an instant, of the Adi-Buddha. The Kangi-ten cult had divine sanction, or so it seemed, and it was formally and unquestionably established.

In brief, Kangi-ten represents the Union of the soul of the Universe, with the Primordial Essence, in feminine form, the soul of the Universe being the Adi-Buddha, Variochana. Its rituals, however, were secret and exclusive and were never thrown open for general participation. It remained a mystery.

With this, Ganesha's journey abroad ends. He has changed form and substance considerably but through all those vicissitudes he kept his elephant head and it remained largely unbowed. As his powers waned, away from his natural habitat, he seemed to escape into the occult and the mysterious, maintaining a distance from the congregational worshipper, holding him at arm's length, never coming out in the open. In contrast, in his own homeland, he became even more accessible, worshipped privately and publicly with equal fervour. Ganesha, true god of the people, put there by popular vote, has taken, in fact, to the streets, at least in one Indian city, Bombay.

*Japanese form. Porcelain, 19th century.*

Yantras are mystical diagrams which have their own elaborate rules of geometry, symmetry and colour. They are part of a highly specialised mode of worship. Each *yantra* is a symbol in which the deity to be invoked lies dormant, waiting to be aroused, or brought into existence, by *sadhana,* the effort of contemplation. Sadhana employs *mantra* or incantation as prime instrument. Once the deity is aroused, the *yantra,* for the duration of that ceremony, becomes the deity, its body.

The whole process is highly internalised. The worshipper or *sadhaka* first arouses the deity in himself and then transfers the divine presence or Self thus activated to the *yantra*. The *yantra* is then 'installed' much as an idol is installed in other *pujas* by infusing it with *prana*, vital breaths. It has been externalised or imaged in order to facilitate worship.

There are different designs for deities but all *yantras* are enclosed in a square that excludes or shuts them off, symbolically, from the outside world. They have openings, however, to regulate the inflow of selected forces. *Yantras* are exclusive enclosures, so to say, within which the deity functions for the sole benefit of the worshipper. He is trapped in the *yantra* by the worshipper through the power of meditation.

This is the tantric way. Contrary to popular misbelief, *Tantra* is not just a set of malefic practices running counter to the sanctified Vedic path to salvation. It is a whole, complex philosophy of worship which could be either used or misused. Like any other human agency, it is a double-edged weapon. Only, perhaps, with sharper cutting edges.

*The Ganapati Bhadra Yantra concentrates on Ganesh and is a geometric configuration of seventeen vertical and seventeen horizontal lines and the squares that these form. The border of while, red and black bands stands for the three qualities that determine character and proclivities — sattva, rajas and tamas.*

आवाहनं न जानामि न जानामि विसर्जनम् ।
पूजां चैव न जानामि क्षम्यतां परमेश्वर ॥
मन्त्रहीनं क्रियाहीनं भक्तिहीनं सुरेश्वर ।
यत्पूजितं मया देव परिपूर्णं तदस्तु मे ॥

*Invitation or its ways I know not*
*Nor even how to say farewell*
*My puja done in ignorance*
*Awaits forgiveness, Lord of Lords:*
*Leaving much to be desired*
*Lacking mantras, rites, devotion*
*Lord of Lords, what I submit*
*Make perfect with your touch of grace.*
— Prayer from a Ganesha puja

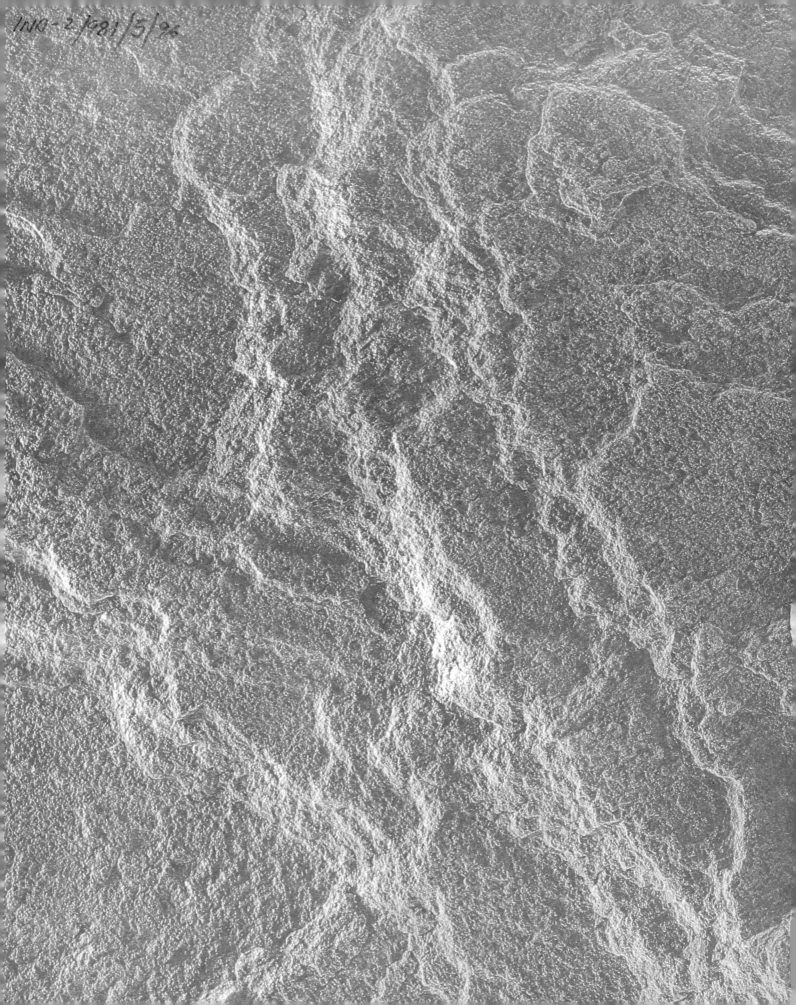